When Hope Breaks

Finding Faith in the Depths of Infertility Grief

CINDY REMO TAN

Copyright.

This book is dedicated to my beautiful adopted daughter,
Carabelle Jeng-An Tan. She inspires me to keep growing, makes me laugh
to lighten the darkness and teaches me to trust the "God Plan".

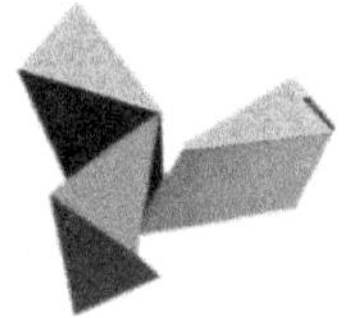

CONTENTS

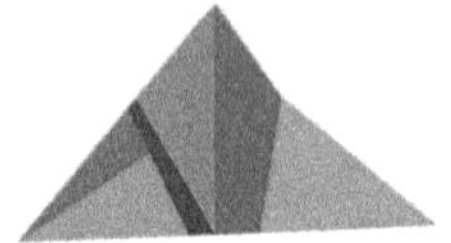

Acknowledgment

To my dear friend and mentor, Peter Vassallo,

Your unwavering support over the past two decades has been a gift I will cherish forever. Thank you for lending your sharp eye and thoughtful insights to this book, shaping it with your wisdom and skill.

Your constructive feedback and constant encouragement not only for this book - breathed life, even when I felt I had nothing left to give.

You have not only been an exceptional editor but also a steady source of inspiration and guidance throughout my career journey. Your belief in me has been a light on the days when doubt loomed large.

Peter, your kindness, patience, and dedication to excellence have left an indelible mark on my life. This book is stronger because of you, and I am forever grateful for your friendship, mentorship, and faith in the message it carries.

With heartfelt appreciation,

Cindy R. Tan

Preface

From the moment she cradled that "Baby Alive" doll in her tiny arms, her heart knew its deepest desire.

At just eight years old, she wasn't merely playing house; she was rehearsing a dream etched into her soul. She'd carefully feed the doll, tenderly change its nappies, and even retreated to her room to nurse it as if it were real.

Being a mum wasn't just a childhood whim—it was a calling that whispered within her - a hope that danced through her every day.

However, this dream became a challenging journey, a nightmare even - leaving her with a deep sense of longing.

A journey that would lead her through the labyrinth of infertility grief, where the seas of longing and loss crashed against the shores of her soul with unrelenting force.

Welcome to "When Hope Breaks: Finding Faith in the Depths of Infertility Grief". Embark through the dark waters of infertility grief, held together by faith and maybe a few cups of tea.

In this book, we'll delve into the raw emotions, heart-rendering experience, and profound questions that accompany the struggle to conceive, the feeling of a missed blessing.

From the empty ultrasound room to the bittersweet joy of adoption, we'll explore the complexities of longing for a child while grappling with the deep ache of unfulfilled dreams.

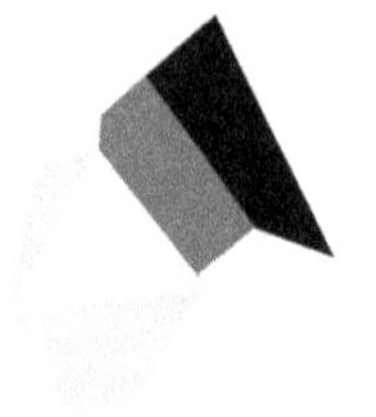

Chapter 1

The Heartache of Empty Ultrasound Rooms

There's nothing quite like the emotional ride of endometriosis check-ups and ultrasound scans.

For most people, these are just routine medical appointments. But for those of us walking the path of infertility, they feel more like stepping into the ring for another round of an exhausting fight, where hope and heartbreak take turns landing blows.

In the beginning, each visit holds that small, flickering light of possibility — a "maybe this time" moment — only to be met with the crushing weight of reality when the screen shows nothing but an empty womb and disease.

The cold gel, the sterile room, the quiet hum of the machine — they all feel like part of a cruel ritual. You clutch that paper gown around you like it's a flimsy shield against the disappointment you know might come.

When the ultrasound tech quietly clicks through the images and says nothing, your heart beats louder than the hum of the machine, and you find yourself whispering, "Please, God, not this again." And the truth is, this isn't a one-time thing. For those of us suffering with endometriosis, ultrasounds are just part of the landscape. They're ongoing, relentless.

The vision of an empty womb becomes like an unwelcome houseguest who just won't leave. It's a constant, unwanted reminder that this battle is far from over.

Year after year, scan after scan, it becomes clear that this cycle of lost dreams and despair is an unending loop. And you become numb, both physically and emotionally.

You try to brace yourself each time, telling yourself you're prepared, you're over it, but the sight of that blank screen always finds a way to cut just as deep as it did the first time. It's a kind of grief that never quite settles, always finding new ways to catch you off guard.

So, what do we do with this?

How do we live in the tension of longing for something that may or may not come? We let ourselves feel the pain without pretending it doesn't exist. Because in the end, we're not here to be perfect or to have all the answers. We're here to hold on to hope, even if we have to do it with tired hands and a few tears.

Chapter 2

Let's Play Pretend

Oh, the pursuit of perfection – that glittering, mirage-like finish line that always seems just out of reach. It's funny how, in the midst of grief, we start playing this odd little game.

We tell ourselves that if we can just make everything 'look' perfect on the outside, maybe, just maybe, we'll start to feel better on the inside. So, we throw ourselves into this new project: making everything appear flawless.

We become experts in our chosen craft: meticulous homemaking. We curate Pinterest boards with themes like "Minimalist Meets Rustic Farmhouse," and we rearrange the throw pillows so many times that even they start to look a little overkill.

We think, "If I can just get this room, this outfit, this Instagram post 'just right', maybe I'll start to feel whole again."

And don't even get me started on the subject of social media.

We craft captions that read like inspirational quotes from a very emotionally stable person, and we post photos filtered to the nines, making our lives look like a highlight reel from a feel-good movie. But deep down, we know it's all smoke and mirrors, a beautifully constructed facade meant to distract not just everyone else, but ourselves, from the truth.

Because here's the thing about facades: they're hollow. The ache remains, no matter how artfully we paint over it. It lurks beneath every curated photograph, every perfectly presented meal, and every blissful-looking holiday selfie.

We discover that no amount of faux-perfection can fill the void or quiet the gnawing pain inside. But still, we try. We hustle for this false sense of security, thinking that if we can control these little pieces of our lives, we might just stave off the heartbreak.

It's tempting to think that maybe, if we perfect all the things we 'can' control, we'll be okay with the one thing we can't. Spoiler alert: it doesn't work that way.

You might look good doing it, but eventually, you're going to trip, fall, and be left wondering why you thought this was a good idea in the first place.

And when you're on the ground, breathless and bruised, you realise that perfection was never really the goal; it was just a distraction from the pain, a desperate attempt to make sense of something that defies understanding.

But here's the good news: God never asked us for perfection. He says, "Come to me, all you who are weary and burdened, and I will give you rest." — Matthew 11:28. Maybe it's time to let go of the pursuit of perfection, and embrace the rest.

To stop hiding behind the carefully curated facade and admit that it's okay to not be okay.

Because here's the secret: true fulfillment, true peace, doesn't come from getting everything just right. It comes from being real – with ourselves, with others, and most importantly, with God.

12.

Chapter 3

A Father's Dream Deferred

There are moments in life that feel like they're written in indelible ink, scenes that play over and over again in your mind, like a movie reel that won't stop spinning.

For me, one of those scenes starts with my dad, sitting at the kitchen table, his eyes sparkling with that familiar mix of hope and impatience. He was a man of few words, but when he spoke about wanting to be a grandfather, his voice held a tremor of longing.

"Why not try IVF?" he'd ask, with that gentle persistence that always seemed to win me over eventually. "There's always a way, you know. You just have to keep trying." But I would shake my head and offer the same excuse: "Not yet, Dad. The timing isn't right. The business needs me focused right now. Soon, I promise."

"Soon" turned into months, and months turned into years. All the while, my dad would drop gentle hints—comments during our catch-ups, knowing glances across the dining table, I knew he just wanted to be a granddad and a great one at that. I kept telling myself there would be time, it'll come naturally - in God's timing. Time to focus on the business now which God has blessed us with, to build something solid, and then, the family will come.

But life, as it often does, had other plans.

The cancer diagnosis came swiftly, a thunderclap on a clear day. There was no warning, no chance to brace for impact. In an instant, the world seemed to tilt on its axis, and everything that once felt important was suddenly rendered meaningless. I remember sitting beside his hospital bed, holding his hand as he slept, his face a pale shadow of the strong man I'd always known. The urgency in his voice, the quiet yearning in his eyes—all of it came crashing down on me in waves, over and over again.

And there it was: the perpetual torment of the "what if." What if I hadn't waited? What if I'd listened to him sooner? What if I hadn't been so focused on my career, my ambitions, my plans? Every time I closed my eyes, I saw him, not in his final moments, but sitting at that kitchen table, still waiting for news that would never come.

He didn't live to see us try. He didn't live to hold his grandchild in his arms or to hear the laughter of a little one calling him "Opa".

14.

And that grief—it feels like it sits on my chest every single day, pressing down with the weight of a thousand regrets.

There were days when I felt like I couldn't breathe, like every choice I'd made had somehow betrayed him, had taken away his last, greatest dream. I'd replay the conversations in my mind, trying to find some comfort in his voice, but all I'd hear were his words, encouraging us to keep going, to try, to never give up.

Each time, the words would twist like a knife, reminding me of the time we no longer had. And yet, in all this, there was a strange, small comfort.

My dad never quite understood the idea of adoption. For him, the idea of family was deeply rooted in blood, in the passing down of names and traits, in the stories told by genetics as much as by words. He loved deeply, but he saw things in black and white, and to him, adopting a child was not the same as having one of our own.

So, in a way, I was spared the pain of explaining to him that we had no choice but to choose a different path. I didn't have to see the disappointment in his eyes or hear the confusion in his voice.

He didn't have to grapple with the idea that his future grandchild might not share his kind eyes or his easy laugh. And for that, I was grateful. At least in this, I hadn't failed him.

But even this small comfort tastes like a bitter pill. Because while I didn't have to endure his disapproval, I would have given anything to have him here, to watch him try to understand, to see him come around in his own time, the way he always did when it came to things that mattered most.

I would have taken the awkward conversations, the debates, the quiet disagreements—if it meant I could still pick up the phone and hear his voice and read his sweet, fatherly messages.

And so, I live in this in-between place—a place where the grief is raw and real, but where there's also a flicker of peace in knowing that at least he didn't have to navigate this new reality, that he was spared from something that would have been hard for him to understand.

I miss him every day, and some days the loss feels almost unbearable. But I also know that he loved me fiercely, that he wanted nothing more than our happiness, however it came.

And so, I hold on to that.

I hold on to the idea that with him accepting Christ into his heart before he passed, he would see things differently through the eyes of Jesus and would have accepted the path we chose, to love the grandchild that came into our lives not by blood, but by a different kind of miracle.

I sit here now, looking back at all those moments, I try to remind myself that he understood love in its deepest, truest form. That's what gives me the strength to keep going, to keep believing that there's still something beautiful ahead, even if it's different from what we all imagined.

16.

Chapter 4

Adoption
Not by Blood, But by Grace

Adoption. It's one of those words that holds a whole lot of beautiful promise in its eight little letters. And let's not kid ourselves—it is beautiful. It's profound. It's an act of love that reaches deep into the soul, a true gift. But, like most things in this journey through infertility, it's also a bit complicated.

There's immense joy in welcoming a child into your heart, yet it's tinged with a grief that defies words. Because no matter how much you adore your adopted child (and you do, with every fibre of your being), there's a corner of your heart that still aches for the child you never conceived. The one who might have had your crooked smile or your husband's eyes.

It's a unique kind of grief—one that makes you feel both full and hollow at the same time, like carrying a bouquet of roses with thorns that somehow always manage to prick you.

And then there's the impostor syndrome. The gnawing, quiet voice that asks, "Am I really a mum?" or "Do I deserve to feel like one?" Even as you rock your child to sleep or kiss their scraped knees, there's this sneaking feeling that maybe you're not quite enough. Maybe you're somehow less of a mother because you didn't carry this child in your womb. Maybe the world's definitions of what makes a "real" mum have seeped in more than you'd like to admit.

It's not that you don't love your child fiercely—you do. It's just that sometimes, in the dark of night or when your child innocently says, "Mummy, let's pretend I was in your tummy and you gave birth to me," the grief and disappointment of what cannot be, creeps in. You wonder if you're doing your very best, if you're worthy of this title you longed for so deeply.

You worry that your grief for the child you never had, makes you somehow ungrateful for the miracle in your arms. It's a complex dance of love and longing, feeling fully blessed yet secretly wondering if you're enough and not a total fake.

And while everyone around you talks about the miracle of adoption (and it is a miracle), there are those moments when you're quietly, secretly mourning the miracle that never was.

The part of you that still grieves for the journey you thought you would take, the one where you'd pass down not just your values and traditions but also your genes. It's a feeling few understand but many feel deeply – like a shameful, dirty secret.

18.

And then… there are moments that take that grief and drag it into the light, raw and fresh.

It was during the process of my daughter's adoption—my miracle, my redemption song—that I was required to undergo a full medical examination. Routine. Standard. Expected. Among the tests? A pregnancy test.

I nearly laughed through the pain. How many times had I stared at one line since we started trying at the age of 29? How many times had I thrown away yet another test, another month, another silent disappointment?

But that day… that day was different. The test came back faintly positive. For the first time in my life, a second line.

I stared at it in disbelief, a rush of panic and hope crashing into each other like waves in a storm. Could it be? After all these years? Was this the twist in the story, the impossible now made possible?

I had to wait 24 hours to test again. Twenty-four hours of trembling. Twenty-four hours of daring to believe. Twenty-four hours of bargaining prayers. I felt like I was standing at the edge of a cliff with my arms outstretched, hoping the wind would carry me instead of crush me.

And then, the retest came back.

Negative.

False positive.

False hope.

It was as if the heavens had opened only to mock me—one last time. As if grief needed to remind me that it still had the final word. I wept like I hadn't in years.

The trauma ran deeper than I expected. That faint second line was not just a chemical error—it was a cruel echo of all the years of yearning, a flash of what I had begged God for, only to have it vanish like a vapor.

On the day of handing in the signed adoption papers, I had to smile. I had to show up and be "fit to parent" while still bleeding from a wound no one could see.

That's the part no one tells you about. That sometimes, even in your moment of becoming a mother—finally—a fresh wound opens. One last wave of grief you didn't see coming.

Because infertility doesn't just quietly exit the room once adoption enters.
It lingers. It always finds a way to remind you of the road you never got to walk.

But here's what I'm learning to believe: both can be true. I can grieve and be grateful. I can mourn the biological child I never had, while fiercely loving the one I am chosen to raise. I can hold both sorrow and joy in the same breath—and still be a good mother.

You don't have to prove your worthiness or silence your grief to be a good parent. Being a mother isn't about biology; it's about showing up every day with love, even when it's complicated, even when it's messy. So, if you're struggling with those feelings of being an impostor, take heart.

You are not alone. You are not a fraud. You are a mother, beautifully and wonderfully chosen, in all the ways that truly matter.

And remember, God sees you—in every doubt and every tear—and He knows that your heart, with all its scars and hopes, is exactly where it should be: right here, full of love.

20.

A Prayer for the Mother Who Waited, Wept, and Was Chosen

Dear Heavenly Father,
You see the places in our hearts that still ache.
You know the stories we carry — of hope deferred, of tests taken,
of prayers whispered through tears and dreams we've had to lay down.

Lord, thank You for the child You placed in my arms,
even as I grieve the one I never carried in my womb.
Thank You for choosing me to mother — not through biology,
but through a deeper kind of love that mirrors Your own.

When the past creeps in and the "what-ifs" swirl around me,
remind me that I am not a second-best mother.
Remind me that You don't make mistakes.
You saw every heartbreak, every empty test, every silent night filled with longing
— and You were with me through it all.

On the days when the wound reopens, when I feel like a fraud,
when joy and sorrow tangle in my chest
— give me grace, Lord, to breathe, to rest, to be held.
Help me to stop striving to be "enough" and remember I already am,
because You said so.

Let this motherhood—this messy, miraculous, God-ordained motherhood
— be a testimony that You still bring beauty from ashes.
That You turn false starts into real miracles.
That love doesn't need a DNA match to be holy.

Thank You for seeing me, for choosing me,
and for walking with me — every sacred, complicated step of the way.

In Jesus' name,
Amen.

Chapter 5

Mother's Day

Ah, Mother's Day.

The day that Hallmark and brunch spots eagerly anticipate, and the day that makes some of us want to hide under the covers until it passes. While others are enjoying flower bouquets and sticky kisses from their little ones, you may find yourself scrolling through social media, feeling a mix of envy, grief, and a bit of "why me, God?" thrown in for good measure.

It's a day when the ache of infertility cuts deeper, a relentless reminder of the emptiness you carry. As the world celebrates motherhood, you're left grappling with the deafening silence of dreams unfulfilled. You put on a brave face, smiling through the pain, but inside, your heart is crying out, "Empty Womb." The absence is more than a void—it's a weight, a relentless ache that whispers you may never feel the warmth of tiny newborn fingers curling around yours, flesh of your flesh, blood of your blood.

And when well-meaning comments like, "You're still an adoptive mother," or "There are other ways to be a mum," reach your ears, they feel like salt on an open wound.

It's okay to want to scream. It's okay to feel inadequate, lost, or even angry.

Because truthfully, no one prepares you for this excruciating longing that grips your soul—a longing for a life you might never hold.

In my early twenties, I carried a promise that felt as certain as sunrise. I believed God had spoken directly to me through His Word. I remember the verse so clearly: "The fruit of your womb will be blessed…" — Deuteronomy 28:4. I underlined it. I dated it. I circled it in hope. I believed it was mine.

I prayed it on my knees. I whispered it through tears. I held onto it through every negative test, every sterile appointment, every month that ended the same way. When disappointment came, I clung tighter. You said, Lord. You said the fruit of my womb would be blessed.

Years passed.

Then more years.

And the promise, at least as I understood it, did not unfold.

I never wanted to say it out loud — the thought felt almost dangerous — but deep down I wrestled with the question that terrified me: Had God broken His promise to me? Scripture says He does not lie. He does not fail. So if something had gone wrong, surely it was me.

Maybe I misread.

Maybe I misunderstood.

Maybe I claimed something that was never meant to be claimed the way I claimed it.

And slowly, something inside me shifted. The verse that once felt like a love letter began to feel like a wound. Instead of comfort, it stirred confusion. Instead of confidence, it birthed fear. I became cautious with Scripture, almost afraid to cling too tightly to another promise in case I misunderstood again. I didn't stop loving God. But I did start approaching His Word with trembling hands.

It's a strange trauma — not losing faith in God, but losing trust in your own ability to hear Him correctly.

And yet, somehow, in the depth of this despair, there's permission to grieve, to be vulnerable, and to hold space for the hope that feels so impossibly far away.

Your body feels like it has betrayed you, and in this betrayal, you find yourself waiting on the Lord. But we wait because we are broken, and somehow, we are broken because we are waiting. It's a paradox that stretches the soul, a test of faith that feels unrelenting.

So, on days like these, let's give ourselves permission to feel whatever comes — to be exactly where we are. Whether that means celebrating quietly with those in your inner circle, staying in with a good book, or driving with the windows down and the music up, know this: God sees you.

He sees your longing, your grief, your questions you're almost afraid to voice. He sees the verse you once clung to and the tears that followed. He sees the hope that stubbornly refuses to die, even after it has been bruised.

And on this day, like every other, He holds you close, even when the answer to "why" seems far away.

24.

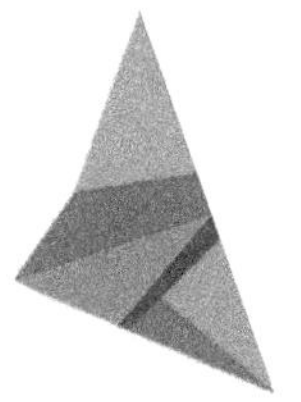

Chapter 6

When Birthdays Become a Bruise

*"He heals the brokenhearted and binds up their wounds." – Psalm 147:3**

There was a time when birthdays felt like a celebration—a joyful pause to reflect on life's blessings, a marker of growth and new beginnings. But something shifted the year I turned thirty-nine.

I had started exploring IVF at the age of thirty-five, after years of trying and waiting in hopeful expectation. What began as cautious optimism quickly turned into devastation. In those sterile clinic rooms, beneath the harsh lights and clinical charts, came a diagnosis I never saw coming—early menopause.

Words that felt like a guillotine, slicing through every tender hope I still clung to. While my friends were still planning families, I was being told that my body was winding down. Too soon. Too fast. Too final.

I remember the disbelief. The numbing silence that followed. The shock of hearing that I wasn't just "delayed" or "taking longer"—I was already running out of time.

Hormones were failing. Follicles were disappearing. Options were shrinking. Hope, once vibrant and prayer-soaked, began to wither under the weight of medical facts I couldn't change.

And yet, I kept going. After years of trying, testing, praying, and clinging to faith through clenched fists, I found myself sitting across from several fertility specialists, some, who looked me in the eye and said it was time to let go. "It's a lost cause unfortunately for you.

We might be able to harvest at best 10 eggs and then maybe 3 might take" one said with clinical coldness. "Take the $15,000 you would have spent on IVF and book yourselves a nice holiday with your husband. Go and enjoy your life."

He said it like he was offering kindness. But to me, it felt like a funeral—like they had pronounced the death of a dream I had nurtured since I was a little girl cradling a plastic doll, believing one day I'd hold a real baby of my own.

Ever since, birthdays have carried a different weight.

26.

They no longer feel like a gift wrapped in ribbon and laughter. Instead, each year has become a silent reminder of what is slipping further out of reach. The candles on the cake flicker like tiny flames of grief, dancing in mockery of the dreams I once held with open hands.

The calendar's cruel consistency keeps coming—year after year—each birthday whispering, "Another year gone. Still empty."

It's hard to explain this kind of sorrow. The world celebrates your life, not knowing that inside, you are mourning the lives that will never be. The silence is deafening, because how do you tell people that your heart is breaking over a womb that's gone quiet too soon?

That the balloons and cards only deepen the ache? You smile for the photos. You eat the cake. But inside, you're screaming into the void, "This isn't how it was supposed to be."

And yet—even here—Jesus sits with me.

In the quiet of my birthday morning, before the messages start rolling in, I bring Him my sorrow. I let the tears fall freely, knowing He understands the language of my grief. I lay before Him the pieces of another year lost to longing, and I feel His gentle presence remind me: "I see you. I know. I'm still writing your story."

He doesn't rebuke the pain. He doesn't rush me out of it. Instead, He holds space for it. For me. Because healing is not about forgetting—it's about finding Him in the wound.

So each year, as the candles are lit, I whisper a different kind of prayer—not for what I've lost, but for the grace to carry the loss with courage.

Not for the miracle I once begged for, but for eyes to see the miracles that still unfold around me. And for a heart that trusts that even this—especially this —is being redeemed.

Maybe birthdays will always sting a little.

Maybe they'll always remind me of the children who never were. But they also remind me of the One who never left. The One who binds up the broken and breathes beauty into ashes.

And with that, I exhale—softly, slowly—knowing that even if my body has finished its chapter of birth, my soul is still being made new.

28.

Of the Ashes

Cindy—born of cinders, where fire burned deep.

But in God's hands, burning is not the end—it's the beginning.

From scorched earth, new life breaks through.

Grief refines, loss regenerates.

Ashes hold holy promise.

She is not forgotten—she is becoming.

Beauty is rising where flames once raged.

Chapter 7

When the Tide Won't Turn

They don't tell you about the waves.

They don't tell you about the days when grief feels like an unwelcome visitor who keeps knocking at the door, refusing to take the hint. Sure, there are moments when the sun peeks through, and you find yourself thinking, "Maybe today is the day I'll feel okay." But then, just as you're about to take that first breath of relief, the wave comes crashing down again.

Infertility grief is a special kind of heartbreak.

It's not a one-time deal, like a broken bone that heals over time. No, this is the sort of pain that revisits, again and again, in a thousand different ways. It's like trying to have a picnic on a beach, but the tide keeps creeping in, slowly soaking your blanket, chilling your feet, and reminding you that the ocean is still very much there.

And let's be honest — we've all wondered, "Why can't this pain have a little more predictability?" A calendar appointment would be nice.

If only it could say, "Wave of grief expected around 3 p.m. — schedule accordingly." But it doesn't work that way. Instead, it sneaks up on you and you find yourself crying because you'd give anything to have a child that's slightly a mirror image of you.

It comes late at night, when the house is quiet and all the "what-ifs" come out to play. What if I never get over this? What if I cannot accept God's plan for me - the plan I had for myself, of being a biological mother? What if my broken heart doesn't heal? And there it is again — that wave, knocking you off your feet just when you thought you were finding your balance.

Here's the thing about grief: it doesn't ask for permission. It just shows up uninvited - sometimes with the subtlety of a whisper, sometimes like a freight train. And it's okay to be mad about that.

It's okay to feel cheated and confused and desperately tired of it all. But it's also okay to laugh when you can, even if it's the kind of laugh that comes through tears.

There's another layer to this grief that no one warns you about — the way it can build a wall between you and the one you're supposed to love forever.

I want desperately to reach out to my husband, to lean on him in this time of heartbreak, but I see how he, too, has turned inward, unable to handle maybe his own grief. He builds his walls, sweeps his pain under the rug, and leaves me standing on the other side, waiting for a comfort that never comes. It's not that he doesn't care, but maybe his way of coping is to avoid, to pretend that if we don't speak of it, it doesn't hurt as much, it will disappear magically.

And so, I find myself suffering in silence, trapped in a lonely prison, longing for a hand to hold, for a shoulder to cry on, but finding only empty space where his compassion should be.

I think God gets this. I really do. I think He understands the exhaustion of fighting the same battles over and over. And I don't believe for a second that He expects us to handle it all with perfect grace.

Maybe that's why there are so many Psalms that read like someone yelling at the sky, only to circle back to hope by the end. God can handle our frustration, our anger, our loneliness, our messy, unpredictable grief.

So, what do we do when the waves keep coming?

We breathe. We hold on. We find moments of lightness wherever we can — in the friends who don't need us to explain, in the small joys that sneak up on us, in the way the sun feels on our face on a good day. And when the wave crashes again, we let ourselves feel it.

We trust that even when it feels like there's no reprieve, there is still grace enough for us, grace that meets us in the deepest waters. And we remember: the waves may not stop, but neither does God's presence.

He is there, holding us, in every single wave, every single tear, every single laugh that comes despite it all. And maybe, just maybe, that's enough to keep us going when the tide won't turn.

32.

Chapter 8

Finding Hope in Faith

Infertility grief has a way of shaking the very foundation of our faith. It can leave you standing in the ruins of your own heart, staring up at the sky, and asking, "Why, God? Why not us?" It's easy to feel lost, to wonder where you fit in the grand design when the Bible says that children are a blessing from the Lord, yet that blessing feels like it's being withheld.

You hear it often: "God has a plan for you." And in those moments of deepest despair, it's hard to understand what that plan could possibly be.

But then there's Romans 8:28, whispering into the quiet spaces of your doubt: "And we know that in all things God works for the good of those who love Him, who have been called according to His purpose." 'All things' — even this pain, this longing, this season of wondering, waiting and letting go.

There are days when these words feel like a distant echo, hard to grab onto when every baby announcement and someone's baby bump feels triggering and like salt in a wound. But if we lean in, just a little closer, we find a promise embedded there, a reminder that our story is part of a larger tapestry we cannot yet see. God, in His infinite wisdom, is working through even this — not to harm us, but to shape us, to build something beautiful from the ashes of our broken dreams.

And in those moments when the grief feels unbearable, we find solace in the hope that there is a bigger picture, one that stretches far beyond our limited understanding. A picture where every tear is counted, every prayer heard and noted - every heartache known. And we remember that our pain does not go unseen by the One who holds all things in His hands.

Then there is the deeper hope that reaches beyond the here and now, a hope that looks toward a future so bright it's hard to imagine. The Bible speaks of Jesus' second coming, a promise that one day He will return to make all things new. It's a hope that says this world, with all its sorrows and losses, is not the end of our story.

A friend once offered a thought that caught me by surprise and lingered in my heart: "Maybe, in the new righteous world where Jesus reigns, you will have the promise of a child from your womb." It seemed like such an unexpected thought, a tiny flicker of possibility that carried a glimmer of light.

34.

Maybe in that new world, where there is pure righteousness and goodness — where everything broken is made whole — there will be a child, born not in the way we expect, but in a way that reflects God's perfect plan.

A child who would have my smile, my husband's eyes, and whose laughter would echo through the halls of a place where hope and joy reigns.

And so, in the waiting, in the quiet spaces of grief, we hold on to that hope.

We allow ourselves to dream a little, to imagine the unimaginable — that in the new world to come, there is still a chapter waiting to be written. A chapter filled with the deepest desires of our hearts, fulfilled in ways that only a loving and sovereign God can orchestrate.

In this journey, we may not always find the answers we are looking for, but we can find comfort in knowing that God is with us in every step, every tear, every moment of doubt. And we trust that His plans for us, though they may be mysterious and hard to grasp, are ultimately for our good, and His Glory.

So we cling to the promise of His return, when all will be made right, and all our longings will find their true fulfillment.

And until then, we take comfort in the hope that Jesus walks this road with us, holding us close, whispering, "I have not forgotten you. I am working even in this, and I am preparing a place where every desire of your heart will find its perfect home.

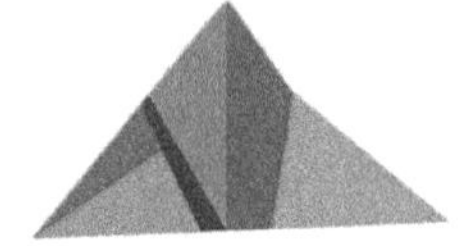

Chapter 9

God's Beautiful Ending

Isaiah 54:1

"Sing, O barren woman, you who never bore a child;
burst into song, shout for joy, you who were never in labor;
because more are the children of the desolate woman than
of her who has a husband," says the LORD.

"When Hope Breaks: Finding Faith in the Depths of Infertility Grief" is more than a recounting of loss and longing.

It's about finding the courage to keep breathing through the heartbreak, to hold on to faith even when it feels like God is silent or distant.

There are days when the pain cuts deep, and hope feels like a cruel joke, but even in those moments, know this: you are not forgotten. You are seen, held, and loved by a God who knows your story from beginning to end.

Infertility isn't a journey anyone would choose, and it's certainly not one that comes with easy answers. It's raw and lonely, ever so lonely and often feels unfair.

Yet, in the middle of this mess, there's a truth we can cling to: God specialises in turning our deepest sorrows into something unexpected — and yes, even beautiful.

Maybe not in the ways we'd planned or imagined, but in ways that reveal His tenderness and grace in every broken place.

And while the road may be long, the waiting hard and the letting go even harder, there is still hope — a hope that God will take this season of grief and use it for something greater than we could have dreamed.

He may not give us the answer we want or in the timing we hope, but He promises to walk with us through every tear, every prayer, and every step forward. And in His time, He will turn what feels like tragedy into a blessing that reaches deeper than we ever thought possible.

So, take heart. You are part of a story much bigger than this moment, and even now, God is writing a beautiful ending that only He can see.

About the Author

Cindy Remo Tan

Cindy is a Christian, shaped by faith - developing resilience through the long road through infertility. She is passionate about giving words to the silent grief many women carry.

After walking her own journey through years of longing, loss, and ultimately adoption, Cindy began writing to offer comfort, honesty, and hope to others navigating similar paths.

She doesn't shy away from the hard questions of faith, but instead leans into them — believing that broken places are often where God's grace shines brightest.

Through her book, Cindy hopes readers feel seen, understood, and reminded that even when hope feels shattered, God is still writing a beautiful story.